www.**rbooks**.co.uk

www.transworldireland.ie

Also by Sister Stan

GARDENING THE SOUL
NOW IS THE TIME
SEASONS OF THE DAY
STILLNESS THROUGH MY PRAYERS

and published by Transworld Ireland

MOMENTS OF STILLNESS

Sister Stan

TRANSWORLD IRELAND

TRANSWORLD IRELAND
An imprint of The Random House Group Limited
20 Vauxhall Bridge Road, London SW1V 2SA
www.rbooks.co.uk

MOMENTS OF STILLNESS
A TRANSWORLD IRELAND BOOK: 9781848270589

First published in 2009 by Transworld Ireland,
a division of Transworld Publishers
Transworld Ireland paperback edition published 2011

A CIP catalogue record for this book
is available from the British Library.

Addresses for Random House Group Ltd companies outside the UK
can be found at: www.randomhouse.co.uk
The Random House Group Ltd Reg. No. 954009

The Random House Group Limited supports The Forest Stewardship Council
(FSC), the leading international forest certification organisation. All our titles that
are printed on Greenpeace approved FSC certified paper carry the FSC logo. Our
paper procurement policy can be found at www.rbooks.co.uk/environment

Typeset in 12/16pt Granjon by Falcon Oast Graphic Art Ltd.
Printed in the UK by CPI Cox & Wyman, Reading, RG1 8EX.

2 4 6 8 10 9 7 5 3 1

Mixed Sources
Product group from well-managed
forests and other controlled sources
www.fsc.org   Cert no. TT-COC-2139
© 1996 Forest Stewardship Council
FSC

Contents

Acknowledgements

I wish to express my appreciation and gratitude to Treasa Coady, Sile Wall and especially Siobhan Parkinson, who encouraged, supported and assisted me with the various drafts of this book and helped me to bring it to completion.

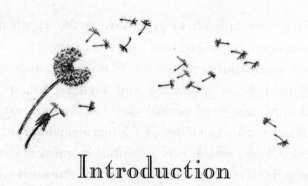

Introduction

I remember the first time I heard the dawn chorus. I was about twelve years old, and I stood at the back of the house, beside the river, where the montbretia and the fuchsia were in full bloom against mountain ash and oak trees. The glorious song of a multitude of birds broke over me, and in a moment that is still alive for me today, it was as if I had never heard birds singing before. I began to wonder if they always sang like that and I just hadn't noticed. As I stood and listened to the birds pouring out their song above me, and gazed at the beauty around me, it felt as if the day grew brighter and brighter and everything around me grew still. In fact, in those few moments, time seemed to stand still and I remember the feelings of awe and wonder which took me over. It was as though I was standing in the presence of something very special, something beyond sacred.

It is very difficult to express what this experience meant to me, but when I look back at it I know it was one of the most significant moments of my life – a very special moment of awareness and mystery, for, quite suddenly, this very normal day had become extraordinary to me. And although I forgot about it for many years, I know now it was a spiritual moment too, one which drew me into a stillness that has remained with me. Right through my life, wherever I have lived, in the country or in the middle of the city, and no matter what the demands and the pressures of life, I have always sought out opportunities to experience moments of stillness, to access that special peace. Indeed, I wrote this book in the Sanctuary, a spirituality centre which offers space and silence, stability and stillness, to all who come here, and which is located in the heart of Dublin.

I feel blessed and so lucky to have had the chance to experience nature in all its glory at this young age, for I'm aware that young people are rarely still long enough to heed special moments such as this. Bursting with energy, and with so many 'things' to do, young people often fail to notice these precious moments.

For me, nature provided the opportunity to connect with stillness, but the world of art, music or poetry can also have this effect. Even a sudden loss, or illness, can bring new meaning to our lives, for we are taken out of the everyday world and our attention focuses on the other world that is always present but not always seen. It is as though a curtain is raised and we see things clearly for the first time; we know that there is another dimension to our existence.

Moments of stillness are so very important because they can bring incredible gifts of understanding. If we allow ourselves the time to be still, matters of concern can often be brought into perspective and we see more clearly the path ahead or the solution to a problem. It is at times like this that we come face to face with reality and, free from the constraints of time, we get a glimpse of the eternal order beneath it. We may see ourselves no longer as isolated individuals, but in communion with everyone and everything; we experience ourselves as part of the whole of creation, not just human life, but all the life of the planet, past, present and future.

This book is an attempt to share with you my moments of stillness beyond thought, beyond the activity of the mind. The book does not set out to give you information or to convince you about anything. It is not about bringing you ideas that your mind can play around with or analyse, criticize or agree or disagree with. It is simply intended to bring you into the stillness that lies deep within you – a stillness that is always present and always accessible. And if you struggle with the meaning of stillness, please stay with this book – give it a chance to unlock the gifts within. For it is only by being still that you will gain a true understanding of stillness and all that it has to offer you. The remarkable thing is that a glimpse of stillness, such as my dawn chorus moment many years ago, can be the beginning of an experience that lasts for ever. That glimpse might come when you are reading this book.

Stillness comes about through inner silence, but it is so much deeper than the emptiness of silence. As you drop through the silence, you come to a stillness which is full of presence.

This is not a book to be read sequentially. It is a book to be lived with. Read a meditation or an aphorism, and allow it to move you beyond thought into that place within where you can be truly still. I don't expect this book will teach you anything new in terms of thoughts or ideas, for the words written here are merely pointers that may lead you to a place that is much deeper than thought. But I hope that the short reflections here will lead you to a still point where, as Thomas Merton says, 'God has written his name on us.'

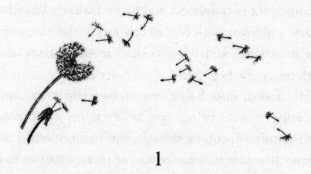

1

The Natural World

Moments of stillness
moments of silence
nourish our relationship
with the whole of life

I grew up in the Irish countryside, in the shadow of the mountains and near the sea. On summer nights, a group of us children would gather together and spread a rug in a field of new-mown hay. Lying on our backs, we would wait for the sky to darken and the stars to come twinkling out. We lay there enraptured by the fragrance of the hay, listening to the singing of the birds, the strange rasping cry of the corncrake from the bog, the voices of frogs from the river and the flow of the river itself. I treasure the memory of those bright summer evenings of my childhood, and I now realize – though of course I did not think of it in this way at the time – that this experience laid down a deep spiritual foundation with me.

Still today, I find that one of the richest and most enduring sources of my spirituality is my relationship with nature. Spending time in the natural world and paying attention to it has made me more attentive to all manner of things in my everyday life; even the smallest and most seemingly insignificant things take on new meaning. Perhaps, when we pay attention to nature, we truly notice what we see. This practice of noticing, of focusing and observing, has a way of slowing down the eye that helps us to see more.

Through nature, I first experienced wonder and awe. Even from a young age I found in nature a refuge, a place to get away from the pressures and distractions of ordinary life. Today, I still find nature's beauty inspiring, although I no longer live in the mountains or near the sea. I live in the middle of the city and you might think this sad, for city landscapes are often harsh, unattractive and uninviting. But there is plenty to see right here, and plenty to enjoy. If we think of nature as some wild and idyllic place, we can end up spending most of our lives waiting to get there. The natural world is here – all around us. It is where we are right now, even in the middle of a bustling city.

To me, nature is a form of divine presence, and indeed many of the religions of both East and West agree it is a metaphor for the spiritual life. God is like a rock, or like the sea, or like the rain in the desert, the psalms say. Jesus compares the coming of God's reign to the sprouting of a seed. And Lao Tzu, the Taoist philosopher, compares the flow of water to the soul's progress. I am learning to appreciate that nature is not simply a presence in which God is encountered. Nature is in itself a form of divine presence. In stillness and silence we can experience that God is not intervening from the outside of our world but rather is the primary, creative force that lies behind the whole process of evolution.

There is a deep divide in contemporary consciousness between the human experience and the natural world. We speak of 'getting back to nature' as if we were not part of it. But like the birds, like the clouds, like the breeze, we are part of nature. Indeed we are made of the same stuff as the animals and the trees. The same energy is alive in them as is alive in us. When we see ourselves as separate from the natural world, like the pioneers of the past, we start to think of nature as something we have to conquer. This is the attitude that has led to the destruction of habitats and species all over the world. This lack of respect for the natural world and all that it has to offer us may well lead to our undoing.

When we recognize our own participation in nature,

we realize that our hierarchies and distinctions among different forms of life have their limits. In focusing on the differences, we can easily forget that all life is one. When we harm an ecosystem, we harm ourselves.

If we accept that we are part of nature, then the mystery at work in the depths of our souls and the mystery at work in the natural world become part of the same reality. Just as the experience of communion that is integral to love reveals to us the presence of the divine in what is most deeply human, so too the experience of communion with nature reveals to us the divine presence at the heart of our world.

Each dawn a genesis,
a new beginning,
a resurrection,
a promise

Moving out of darkness
into light

A time to rejoice,
a moment neither dark nor light,
a time to delight

I am a word
spoken out of the heart of the creator,
spoken into the heart of all creation

The night sky –
we are immersed
in immense mystery

The wood teems with life
bursts with energy

I try to name its clearings,
its streams and hedges,
but each naming builds a boundary,
carves out the territory

For what little is known,
more is unknown

Winter rain strikes rocks,
flows down hills,
soaks grass
Pavements overflow with it –
a mirror for the dark grey sky

Morning
birth of colour

Leaf and flower newly risen
out of the night
out of the earth
leave the darkness
without a thought

Snow whitens the world –
a painted landscape
calling me to stillness

Growth happens in the fertile darkness
where the rain falls and the seed opens
no matter how many trample overhead

Eel swims up river
relaxed, alert

A long dark body
silent, elegant,
below the surface

Gathering speed
it disappears seaward

Soundless, gone

The last darkness of night dissipates,
the sun bursts over the horizon –
every day a new miracle –
rarely experienced,
yet always there

Clouds move and change,
lightsome

They darken,
hang still

Till
a miracle comes bursting through

Marvellous

When I was a child
I looked at Mount Brandon,
3000 feet above sea level,
and its sheer immensity amazed me

Now it calms me:
its majesty breaks down my defences,
its stillness quietens me

One evening in Assisi
St Francis was out enjoying the night air,
when he looked up and saw the moon,
huge and luminous,
bathing the entire earth with its radiance

Since no one was outside to enjoy this miracle
   with him,
Francis ran to the bell tower and began ringing
   the bell enthusiastically

When the people came running in alarm,
demanding to know what was wrong,
Francis just called,
from the top of his tower,
'Lift up your eyes, my friends,
and look at the moon'

Creation speaks
to those who hear with their hearts

A world of life
brimming around me
its harmony inviting me
its fellowship awaiting me
its mystery beckoning me
its timeless presence welcoming me
enveloping me
bringing me back to myself

My father would name each hill,
every field and rock,
every twist and turn,
the unbroken history in the farmland names
connecting him to the land,
so that he brought it with him
wherever he went

The darkness before the dawn
is pregnant with new light

Standing on the shore
I am part of the rhythm of the tide

Each wave is a giving and a taking,
impermanence dissolving into permanence
longing into fulfilment

Everything in nature yearns:
weeds pushing up through pavement cement,
baby birds yawning to feed,
the child's eager reach for the breast,
and so our souls yearn for the divine

River
changeless, changing
stable, moving
ancient, new

Endless

The treasures of the earth are free
and full of surprises

The field is cleared,
ploughed and harrowed

The sower walks,
heavy with seed

He passes along the rows,
sowing as he goes,
setting his foot into tomorrow

Gazing, as the pale yellowy buds of the
   camellia opened,
I knew I was unconditionally loved

Stone fonts catch the river's waterfall
spill it again, as it races and laces
to the sea

The journey of the river
is the journey of the soul
meeting divinity as it spills and falls,
feeding itself over and over from its own source

The bounty of the universe begins with the gift of life
and everything that sustains it

Wild grasses bend in the breeze,
ripple over my body,
caress my face,
seed my hair,
fill my nostrils with sweet freshness

One life,
one world,
one heartbeat

Each new morning happens,
lifting us out of darkness,
holding us in light,
touching us with warmth,
opening us to possibilities,
filling us with hope,
the quiet kindness of this new day

Nature:
we are part of it,
living it and breathing it

It is part of us,
encompassing us,
holding us,
in the folds of its hidden heart
its pulse beats within us

The earth speaks in magic – rainbows, waterfalls

The material world is our way to contact the divine,
every tiny little bit of it
a glimpse into the soul of eternity

A flower opens
to morning light
It closes fast its petals
as the light fades:
a daily miracle

The rhythm of life flows on,
part of the song of the universe

Absorbed in sound:
tide ebbing
river flowing
breeze rustling
stream gurgling
bee humming
bird singing
cat purring

In surrendering completely to sound
we discover the sacred stillness beyond

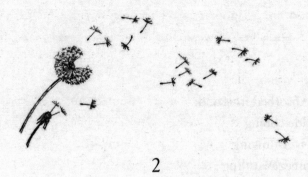

2

Living Life Each Day

Life
is not a drama
made up of scenes around a common theme;
life is a series of experiences
we can use to come to know ourselves better

Life is not what we see happening on the outside.
Whatever we are doing right now is just a mirage; it is
not what we are really doing – it only looks like it. We
only think we are here.

True life is what is happening on the inside, in the
quiet waters of our soul. It is happening all the time,
underneath the job we have to do or the responsibility we
have to see to, the concerns that consume every moment
of our day. And this inner life is driven by energies too

wild for us to ignore. Life is a citadel of time in which we find ourselves, a world we build and create. We live wanting to get it right. We go on searching for the secret of having it all.

We are constantly being tempted and seduced to believe that there is more to life than what we now have; more to life than what is happening at the core of our being. We drive ourselves and each other on in an attempt to reach for the next big 'thing'. The seductive sirens in our head tell us that more is within our grasp, and so we are all constantly striving for an invisible finishing line. We are certain that, once a particular summit is reached, a particular goal achieved, we will be happy at last. And, perhaps understandably, we want our children, our families, to have the best of everything. We want the medal, or the job, or the house or the promotion. We want it badly, we want it now – and we want it for ever. We work to the point of exhaustion to get 'it', or we move listlessly through life, sure of utopia's existence but unsure of how to capture it. We measure ourselves by how closely we can approach it in our lives, or we envy it in someone else's life. We may feel an absence in our lives day and night due to the desire to find it. Its absence makes us aware of our inadequacies, or, if we feel we are achieving it, we may have a sense of superiority as we measure ourselves against others. So, whether we have all that we desire or not, ultimately we are alienated, alone, on the outside of life looking in, and still wanting.

When we live with one foot in tomorrow at all times, plan for tomorrow, prepare for tomorrow, wait for tomorrow, fear for tomorrow, we come to believe that 'here' is never good enough. This moment means nothing. What is now is not important to people on the go. What is coming is always what really counts. What is yet to be seen, yet to be done, yet to be accomplished becomes the essence of life. But if we look constantly ahead, waiting for life, we will find it has passed us by.

We think the problem with life is that time just passes; and because it is out of our grasp and our control we fight against it. In fact, the beauty of life is that it flows, and never stops. It takes us on a journey of twists and turns; life is not lived in a straight line, in a linear fashion. It is an adventure to be experienced, and there is no place for failure because nothing is permanent. Life challenges us and redirects us from one dead end to another until we finally come to see the links between the challenges, the patterns of life and the lessons emerging. And the truth that finally dawns is that life is simply a matter of living – from one season to the next – learning as we go.

Observing where we are, being aware and alert to the moment, is the secret of living well and living fully. It is a lesson that is hard to learn in a culture based on motion. It is not easy to be still in the present moment, to see and fully experience what is in front of us.

I often think the fundamental problem of life is not a lack of opportunity; it is a lack of something else. The Confucians call it righteousness, the Buddhists call it awareness and Christians call it soul; today people refer to it as presence. Life is full of opportunities when we realize that life is here and life is now in this place, in this moment, for each of us to live fully. The present moment lies richly dormant within each of us, waiting to become life.

Life is the primal force
that fuels the universe,
always flowing into us,
blessing us,
flowing through us,
blessing others

Each new day,
as we awaken,
we take a moment to become conscious of who we are,
bringing together the threads of our history,
reminding ourselves where we have come from,
remembering where we are heading to,
what we are drawn to
and why, each day,
we do what we do

When we acknowledge another
with full and unconditional attention
in a moment of alertness
we meet ourselves

Living in hope is
living on the edge between the near and the far
between the finite and infinite
the past and the not yet

Maturity combines the fresh enthusiasm of childhood
with the wisdom of experience

Joy comes in little whispers
in sudden unexpected glimpses of mystery

Memories are a soul pack,
our greatest treasure

Always present,
in any space, in every place

Beginning again,
seeing again the vision that first impelled me,
rediscovering in my heart the magnetism of
    that first call,
capturing again the beauty of my most sacred
    longings,
rekindling and renewing my sense of purpose,
I am drawn willingly and joyfully into life's
    deepest dimensions

It is in responding,
with a full heart,
to the opportunities of each given moment –
no matter how difficult or uninvited –
that we experience joy

Our search is ongoing,
our journey unfinished

The more we discover,
the more we have to learn

Every step on our journey
is a return to the beginning

Divine joy is in us,
given to us out of love,
being born in us anew each day

In learning not to fear uncertainty,
we discover inner strength

I am enough
I am good enough
I have enough

When I know that enough is enough
I will have enough always

Work dignifies our every day,
bringing us further each day into the wonder
   of our journey,
enabling all that is unlived in us
to flower into fullness

The world is ever-created,
each of us still in the making
as each moment we are transformed in love

Our unlived lives,
undreamt dreams,
unloved loves –
our greatest loss in life
is what we allow to die within us
while we live our lives

Life is simple and serene,
full of joy and peace,
when it is lived from the heart
with integrity and truth

The beginning and end of our journey
is finding our true self

In the landscape of my life,
there are places I try to avoid

Still, I lose my way,
and wander off course
into terrain I promised to avoid

You who are the compass of my life,
ease my fear,
and guide my steps,
one by one

Life is not automatic:
we must choose to live it

Unlike other creatures,
we struggle to become who we are,
we experience ourselves as unfinished

Our being is one of becoming:
our glory and our agony

Journeying inward,
into our own powerlessness,
we are in relationship
with the powerless of the world,
and form community with them

Knowing the happiness of an integrated life,
we bring body, mind and spirit into everything we do

Courage is a gift of the heart
It opens us to experience,
urging us to accept and know our pain,
which in turn stirs us to compassion,
melts our hardness,
and frees our creativity

The virtue of lives lived in dependency
of lives lived in the service of others
goes unrecognized

Our humanity calls us
in our poverty and neediness
to make the world a better place

Life is not about giving and taking,
it is about letting go and receiving,
moment to moment

A life of love
is a choice we can make

We all long to feel real,
yet we are afraid to let ourselves become real

We run away from it
even as we are irresistibly drawn to it

Neighbourliness: a sacred gift in a torn world

There is another way to live
in this noisy, distracted world
and it is not as out of reach as it may seem

Wakening to life
is a continuing process

There is no limit to wakefulness:
no one wakes up once and for all

To live from the heart
is to live fully

As we move into our own souls,
releasing the energy of the force of life within
so also we move out to greet the world,
in all its challenges and difficulties,
with peace in our hearts

The purpose of this day is
to discover who we are
and what we are called to be

The purpose of this day is
to find the joy we were born to know,
the person we were born to become

The harvest of our lives is already with us

With every gift
there comes opportunity:
the sun shining through the trees
the dew glistening on an open flower
the smile of a baby
the embrace of a friend

When we take these opportunities,
enjoying them to the full,
we dwell in the gift of being alive

It is only in losing ourselves
by giving to others
that we find our true selves

The wonder moments of life
keep our hearts alive
and sustain and comfort us
in life's heartbreaking experiences

All life is connected at the core,
flowing from the same source,
as it moves and pulses
through our veins
through all beings:
the divine river of life

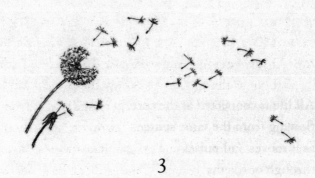

3

Living in the Eternal Now

In the here
in the now
- an eternal moment
gifting us with insight

The 'now' is. It just is. We think we live in time but we only ever live in the 'now', and time is only the possibility of becoming.

As human beings, here and now – not as believers in this or that doctrine – we all know what it feels like to be so distracted that we lose sight of time. But if we can say 'now' and know what we mean by this word, then we are speaking about a free and boundless reality – a reality without restrictions or limits.

We sometimes find it hard to let go of the past, even if

the memories are painful. But why is it that we try to cling to it long after it's gone? Is it because we fear the future? Or do we simply fail to realize that there is really no such thing as the past, there is only the present out of which to make a life? With this understanding, we come to realize that the 'past' cannot harm us, it can only inform us and help us to achieve happier futures. When we connect with the reality of the present moment we give ourselves the chance to learn, to grow and move forward.

Perhaps we find it hard to let go of the past because we feel unable to place our trust in the future. This fear of what lies ahead, this need to control or even force issues, leads us to ignore the 'now' – the precious moment that is so rich in promise and possibility. But life need not be like this – full of tension, anxiety, stress.

The Hindu tradition of spirituality tells us that all we need to do in order to learn to let go of the past is to embrace the future with the knowledge faith gives us of the rightness of the past. Why? Because God is waiting for us here and now, in this new place, in this new moment, just as God has always been there in the past – to give us new insights, to give us new joy.

If the question is 'How can we learn to let go of the past?', the answer is simply that we must surrender the future to the God who created that past and who will accompany us into the future we fear.

Time does not run out

It rises,
as water in a well,
to fullness

Living in the moment
ensures we do not miss the present,
ensures we do not find the day has passed us by
before we have fully lived it,
helps us to greet the night with gratitude,
helps us to welcome death,
when its moment comes

We live in the light of the now
not in the past, in the dark,
not in the brightness of light yet to come

Only here in this moment,
in the mystery of now

Our destiny is here
It is now
It is present

We cannot reach the now
if we think of it in a chronological way

It is here and accessible at every moment
as a mysterious fullness of time

Mindfulness is an inner structure of living consciously, sensitized to the now

It tunes us in to the call of each moment

We do not own time
gain time
save time

All we can do is live in it
and in living in it
move out of it
and into eternity

Bells –
a timeless call to enter the now
to stop
to listen
to hear the message of this moment
and give thanks

Dying daily,
we move naturally into eternal life

We enter into the now
in our most alive moments
and time stands still

Eternity is the overcoming of time
by the now that does not pass away

Living in the now is
an invitation to awaken our soul,
to stop,
to listen,
to choose a different way,
to proclaim harmony and wholeness

When we live in the moment,
we live in and out of time

We are reborn each morning,
into a new time,
a new opportunity to respond
to yesterday's difficulties
in the light of this new day

When we listen to the silence of this moment
we hear the deep desires and longings of our heart

When we let time go,
time is ours

We turn the point between time and now
into creative tension

It is by this inner gesture
that we live life to the fullest

Eternity is in our heart, calling us home

We think we have no time,
we think we are running out of time,
we think time is out of our control

But time is eternal,
and we have all the time we need,
always,
because all time is ours,
now

Each moment
full
always

Lost in doing,
in thinking and remembering,
in planning and anticipating,
we forget how to be ourselves,
to be with ourselves,
>with life,
>where life is,
>in the present,
>in the now

In the present moment, we transcend time

Time,
through which life passes,
is a divine freedom
empowering us now

Feeling unreal
comes from ruminating on the past,
worrying ahead into the future,
not living in the present,
where our real selves reside,
where we are at home

Eternity is not the perpetuation of time,
but is the eternal now

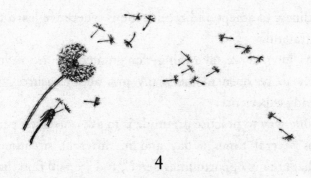

4

Giving Thanks

Thank you
for the ordinary gifts
of every day,
evoking in me
wonder and surprise

The great medieval mystic Meister Eckhart preached that if the only prayer we ever said was *Thank you*, it would be enough.

To be awake, aware and alert is the beginning, middle and end of gratitude. But of course, we cannot even start to be grateful unless we wake up and open our eyes to the colours of surprise that are all around us. When we are awake and open to what is within and around us, we are ready to receive life to the full. This readiness to accept and receive life is where we learn to be grateful.

As long as we take things for granted we are never likely to be open to the many joys and pleasures we already experience.

One way to practise gratitude is to ask ourselves, perhaps several times a day and in different situations, 'What are my opportunities here?', and we will find that at any particular moment the opportunities are huge. There is the opportunity to appreciate and enjoy the gift of sharing, of sounds, smells, tastes, textures, colours and the deeper joys of friendliness, kindness, patience, faithfulness, honesty and all those gifts that soften our hearts.

Working alongside others, sharing and working in partnership with others, also opens up opportunities to be grateful. Grateful that together we can make a difference. Grateful that the simple, even mundane jobs that fill up our day are an important part of the whole. Aware that my 'yes', my 'no' and my 'maybe' all matter, all contribute to creating new surprises, new opportunities for gratefulness. And as you may have discovered, life has many wonderful surprises in store for us.

The most miserable day of cloud and rain can suddenly offer up the most brilliant rainbow; the dull, concrete streets of a town can be brought to life by the sound of children's laughter ringing out in a school playground – the innocence and sheer exuberance can somehow fill the air with energy and life. When we take the time to appreciate wonders such as these, our response can only be one of gratitude.

Surprise can also provide a jolt, enough to wake us from the daze that can fall upon us as we journey through life. For it is surprise that opens our inner eye to the fact that everything is a gift. Since everything is a gift, nothing can be taken for granted. And if it can't be taken for granted, then we must be grateful. As we begin to be grateful, our gratitude grows and grows like expanding ripples on the surface of a pool.

If we practise being awake to surprise and are aware of opportunities at hand, we will spontaneously be alert in our response and we will spontaneously be grateful. We all have millions of opportunities each day to be awake and aware, to be surprised, to give thanks.

When we wake in the morning we may greet the day that lies ahead and acknowledge that this is not just another day; it is the one day that has been given to us, and it is a gift that is given right now. The only appropriate response is one of gratitude. If we try to respond as if it were the first day of our life or the last day of our life, then we will spend that day gratefully, and fully attuned to the many bounties it has to offer us. It need take only a moment or two each morning to simply stop, think and appreciate the fresh possibilities that lie ahead at this unique moment in time. What a wonderful gift!

Gratitude helps us to see things in relative terms, to see the right relationship between things more easily. Gratitude is indispensable on the way to maturity; it dignifies and celebrates life and includes trust.

We can all learn to let our sense of surprise be triggered by the extraordinary but above all by a fresh look at the ordinary. 'Nature is never spent,' says Gerard Manley Hopkins. 'There lives the dearest freshness deep down things.' The surprise of the unexpected will wear off, but the surprise of freshness never wears off.

Turning back to nature, think of the sky. When we look up at it, we are usually only checking the weather. And yet, with constantly changing cloud formations and light, it is different every moment. What a miracle to behold! Right now, at this moment, the sky is unique. Opening our eyes to the sky we can be constantly surprised.

In the same way, if we open our eyes to the faces around us, each face has its own story and each face carries also the story of its ancestors. Every person is coming to us with a gift if only we open our heart to the gift that is being offered.

Then again, think of the everyday things we have in our lives, things we think of as simple and take for granted. Hot and cold running water, for example, and clean sweet drinking water. Millions of people will never experience such luxury, which we think of as a basic necessity.

When opening ourselves to the awareness of the many gifts with which we are showered, we cannot help but respond by blessing. As we open our eyes, we open our hearts and we reach out with a smile or a touch and we let our gratefulness overflow.

When we open our eyes with gratitude
the world is filled with light
and creation announces the divine

Here on every side
in every passer-by
everywhere across the world
and through all time –
the mystery

Praise is our response to glory

The more open we are,
the more the glory shines out

The more we see it shining out,
the more spontaneously we praise

We need to practise waking up to surprise,
by asking ourselves, from time to time,
as we encounter new experiences
or notice everyday ones,
'Isn't this surprising?'

Believing what is not seen,
seeing what is not visible,
knowing the limits of our life,
we give thanks

Giving and taking
are one action in gratitude:
we cannot give thanks
for what we have not taken to heart

Just for ten seconds in silence
remember those who loved the good that grows
    within us,
those who wanted what was best for us,
those who encouraged us to become who we are

Just ten seconds of silence
remembering them
wherever they are

Ten seconds growing in gratefulness –
the heart of prayer

Gratitude is an attitude, not a feeling

It is not enough to feel grateful –
we must think gratefully,
imagine gratefully,
act gratefully

In giving we are replenished
in receiving we give back

Gratitude is like the sun lighting up the landscape:
not a single leaf or blade of grass is different,
but everything looks much more attractive
when we look on it with the eyes of gratitude

Gratitude always gives more
without hesitation

At the core of our being is
emptiness and fullness,
nothingness and everything,
and there dwells the divine

Generosity is contagious

When we allow surprise to flow into our lives,
our whole life becomes transformed
and we take nothing for granted

Gratitude needs to express itself –
the greater our awareness of gratitude
the greater our need to express it

A lighted candle,
flowers on a table –
a meal becomes a feast,
a celebration,
alone or with others,
rejoicing in the fruits of the earth

A grateful heart is a heart filled with joy

Living and working
amongst people who are poor,
amongst people who are lonely,
excluded, marginalized,
ill-treated, homeless,
living with their pain,
their suffering,
their resilience,
their hope,
their belief in miracles

Prophets for today

The child in us never dies
but receives everything with an open heart

Ingratitude blinds us

Not seeing what we have on the way to having more

Not noticing what we step on, on the way to
somewhere else

Not aware of the person beside us on the way to
seeing someone else

Not valuing the good on the way to something greater

Not being in the now on the way to getting ahead

Gratefulness is the ability
to be surprised by the ordinary

Teach me to wait silently,
untroubled and without fear
but full of gratitude and giving thanks

Evening is a time for gratitude
a time to rejoice in life
and count our blessings

We are blessed when we are open
to the gifts of the day

Gratitude is an attitude of mindfulness
making us more alive to what we have received

Sunrise comes unbidden
All is gift
this new day
calling us to gratitude

Surprise cannot be planned or controlled
but it is always there
when we are open to it
and willing to receive it

Just as we see the sun in its rays,
the fountain in its waters,
so may we see streams of divine power
and wisdom in our daily graces and blessings
flowing into our life,
calling us to truth, justice, love and peace

Every moment is given
every moment is gift

The only appropriate response
is gratitude to the giver
for each moment given

At evening, we lift our hearts in gratitude
for the gifts of the day

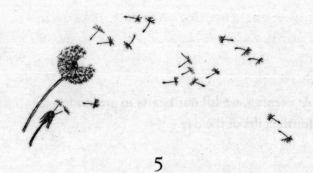

5

Spirituality

God,
ground of my being
mysterious presence
the more I discover you
the more I am

The idea of God has ceased to have meaning for some people, who feel it is a kind of leftover from a half-forgotten mythology. Even people who write about spiritual matters often do not like to use the word 'God', and prefer to speak about 'the absolute', 'the divine', 'a transcendent being', 'creative energy' or simply 'the spirit'. Indeed, I use these terms myself sometimes. But I am not afraid of the word 'God' because, for me, spirituality is about my experience of, and my relationship with, God.

I believe that before God can begin to have any meaning for a person, they have to experience the reality of God in their lives. Arguments will not convert a person to God because God is not a philosophical concept; God is the very centre of our being and we have to encounter God as a fact of our existence before we can truly believe in Him.

To discover God is not to discover an idea, but to discover oneself; it is to awake that part of one's existence which has been hidden from sight and which one has perhaps refused to recognize. Amazingly, for so many, discovering God is like a rebirth, and can make life worth living.

The search for God is an ongoing process, for it seems that the more one discovers, the more one finds one has to learn. Every step forward is a return to the beginning and we will not really know God as God is until we have returned to our beginning and learned to know Him as both the beginning and the end of our journey.

In my own life, the mysterious presence that I responded to in nature as a young girl, which I have described in the introduction to this book, has gradually disclosed itself as the infinite and eternal being, and I have discovered that all the forms of nature are but a passing reflection of His beauty. I also know now the meaning of St Augustine's words, 'O thou beauty, so ancient and so new, too late have I loved thee, too late have I loved thee.'

I have sought and found God in the solitude of nature, in the labour of the mind, in the depth of my being and in prayer, but I have also found Him in people, in community, and in the poor, the needy, the marginalized in our society.

I think of Jesus as the Word of God embracing heaven and earth, and revealing Himself in different ways and under different names and forms to all humanity.

I consider that the Word of God enlightens everyone coming into the world and, though they may not recognize it, it is present in every human being in the depths of their soul. Beyond words and thoughts, beyond all signs and symbols, this Word is being secretly spoken in every heart, in every place and at every time. People may be utterly ignorant of it or may choose to ignore it, but whenever or wherever anyone responds to truth or love or kindness, to demands for justice, or shows concern for others in need, they are responding to the voice of the Word of God. Similarly, I believe that when anyone seeks truth or beauty in science or philosophy, in poetry or art, they are responding to the inspiration of the Word.

For me, the Word took flesh in Jesus of Nazareth and in Him I can find a personal form of the Word to whom I can pray and relate in terms of love and intimacy. But I believe, too, that He makes Himself known to others under different names and forms.

What counts is not so much the name and form as the response from the heart to the hidden mystery which is present in each one of us, in one way or another, and which awaits our response in faith and hope and love.

I also believe that each one of us has an inner light that will lead us through the shadows and illusions by which we are surrounded; this light will open our minds to the truth. For me, the act of meditation, morning and evening every day, is the most direct method of getting in touch with the reality of God. In prayer and meditation I try to let go of everything and listen to the inner voice, the voice of the Word which comes in the silence when all activity of body and mind ceases. Then, in these moments of stillness, I become aware of the presence of God and I try to keep that awareness during the day wherever I am, walking or sitting, driving or on a bus or a train, in work or study, in talking or listening to others. I try to be aware of this presence in everyone and in everything.

So prayer for me is the practice of the presence of God in all situations. In the midst of noise and distractions of all sorts, in the midst of pain and suffering and death, in times of peace and quiet, joy and friendship, alone and with others, in times of prayer and silence, the presence is always there.

A soul touched by the Spirit
is like a tree touched by the sun
It sends forth its buds and leaves,
its blossoms and its fruits,
generous in its gratitude

Stillness finds me
in the smile of a child on the tram
the budding of the cherry blossom at the gate
the sweet scent of the clematis in the garden
the look behind forgiving eyes
the fresh eggs left on the doorstep

Attentiveness to what is enlarges what is

Soul is the unifying energy
at the centre of our being,
never changing
in a constantly changing world

We can never have enough of the divine
because the goodness of the universe is infinite

At birth,
we are all given an angel,
a protection,
a song of courage
And all we need to know
is that it is there

True dignity is never diminished by indifference
or ill will

Absorbed in lighting a candle,
striking the match,
watching the flame flickering into life
and finding the strength to grow,
we enter into the stillness
of that small circle of light

Divine beauty is found in solitude,
it is visible in nature
and it unfolds in the human heart

Relying on divine providence,
living close to the limits of our resources,
we come to an appreciation of the beauty of life,
we come to know that all is gift
and we learn to distinguish necessity from luxury

Only in stillness do we hear truth
Only through stillness do we understand truth
Only out of stillness do we speak truth

Where the poor are, there God is

The soul is that place in us
where love and light,
joy and peace,
truth and beauty
abide

It is a sanctuary,
a holy place,
a divine centre,
to which we may always return

The divine is the depth dimension in human
experience

Awake
aware
beyond thought
pure presence

Journeying in faith
we are who we are in the divine –
no more, no less

We are infinitely more than we imagine,
infinitely greater than our mind

The spiritual life
is a life of love,
of listening and responding,
of giving and receiving

It is never a solo act

Graced moments open us to the transcendent

Living by measurement,
achievement, attainment,
ambition, goals, expectations,
we easily forget how to know
when enough is enough

It takes courage to follow the deepest desires of
    our heart,
to say no to other people's plans for us,
to leave other voices behind
and to say yes to the quiet still voice calling
    from within

A flame burning,
snowflake falling,
bud opening,
wheel spinning –
the dynamic of stillness

Whenever anyone responds to love or kindness,
wherever anyone seeks truth, peace or justice,
there God is

Music arises out of silence
into which it inevitably flows

This is one of the basic laws of life:
we have only what we give up

As we connect,
reconnect and interconnect,
our lives are woven into unity

Divine grace is like a lantern on a dark path
shining only enough to illumine the next step
Only when the next step is taken does the light
   move on

Tomorrow is the enemy of today,
for we cannot be tomorrow
what we can be today

Without love
justice is realism
hope is self-centredness
forgiveness is self-abasement
generosity is extravagance

Connecting with the spirit
we open ourselves to the force of love
that drives the universe

Spirituality integrates and transforms the
material world

So many mornings I saw it from the window
before any other thing
dark against the daybreak
silvery in summer light
its faint outline in fog
remote and serene

I knew it was there and there it would stay
not moving like the tide or river
not shifting like the sand
not changing with the seasons like the trees
its movements imperceptible

It seemed to me to be stability itself
even when I couldn't see it
I knew it would still be there
even if I lived a thousand years

When we journey with awareness,
each event is unique
each step the first step to fulfilment

When we hear the stillness in the heart of the world,
all creation becomes our companion

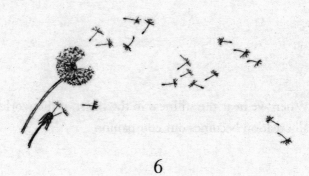

6

Letting Go

In stillness
I notice
people around me,
who they are
who I am
where we are going
how we journey together

Letting go is like dying, but it is dying into freedom. It can be hard to let go – of a thing, a memory, a person, an ambition, an experience, a belief, a thought, an opinion, a position. We are afraid that if we let go of what we know – or what we think we know - we will be lost, unable to find our way back to where we feel secure. But by letting go, we sink into a new security on a different level – one that involves trust, faith, commitment – and welcomes possibilities we could never imagine. Every search, every new question, forms and shapes us, and brings new freedom, new life. Casting off the old which no longer serves us is liberating and important in life's learning process. But it is important, too, to recognize that the unknown can be a frightening place and we, quite rightly, tend to approach it with both uncertainty and caution. For example, in the course of our lives we come across situations where we have to let go, even if we don't want to – when somebody dies, or when somebody leaves or betrays us; we find life overtakes us and we lose control of the known, the familiar. A strange world beckons and unsettles us.

But as uncomfortable as this may be, it is important to recognize that if we try to hang on to the person, the thing that is suddenly out of our grasp, we can become resentful and stuck in the past. We may even be poisoned by a kind of bitter pain that blights our life. In contrast, if we choose to release our grip, move forward and look to the fresh possibilities life offers us each and every day, we can be transformed, reborn and renewed. In this way, painful experiences can be fruitful. They can be an opportunity to grow if only we are prepared to take the risk and let go.

Death, of course, is the ultimate 'letting go'. The finality of death challenges us to be fully present here and now and so begin eternal life. For eternity rightly understood is not the perpetuation of time, on and on, but rather the overcoming of time by the now, that does not pass away.

There is a time to live, as there is a time to die. If we can live with a sense of wholeness that includes death as part of life, we will find death less threatening and illness less fearful. Accepting the inevitability of death and the place of death in the circle of life allows us to stay in the living present, to live a life that focuses on each moment. Taking time to be still, to be aware of precious moments in our day, helps us to accept more easily the inevitability of death. We have, in a sense, absorbed all that life has offered us, all that surrounds us. We have participated in life while realizing that in doing so we are also participating in dying.

If we accept death as part of life, and if we acknowledge that, in a sense, we are dying a little every day, we will not postpone the important things in life: the showing of affection and forgiveness, the kind deed, the loving word. Instead of leaving it until the person's last day when it is too late, when the appreciative word remains unsaid and the good deed unaccomplished, we will do it now, because the time is now. If we express our positive feelings and attitudes, now, today and daily, there will be no regrets when our friends have gone the silent way, there will be no nagging doubts about how things might have been between us.

Denying death is a fruitless and desperate exercise – like trying to hold on to water as it runs through our fingers. Time moves on and life changes whether we like it or not. It seems our youth disappears so quickly, and with it, all too often, our health and even our status in society. But when we learn to accept the inevitability of death, we let go of whatever it is within us that fetters our souls. It may take patience and trust to learn to let go, but that letting go is what living life to the full is all about. Then we may give ourselves to whatever presents itself – fully, completely, without inhibitions. Instead of holding back, we let go and everything is alive. We die into greater 'aliveness'.

To be full,
we must be empty

Letting go of the compulsion
to be successful,
to be right,
to be in control,
to be powerful,
is the way to freedom

We can only take with us when we die
what we let go of when we are alive

It is easier to let God in
when we are broken,
to hear God
when we are stripped empty,
to come close to God
when we have nothing to lose

That is why we need to learn to let go
for in letting go of ourselves
we find God in ourselves,
in our own heart's core

The shining flame of a candle
lights up the things around it

Outside the circle of light
deep darkness lies
limitless:

Divine mystery

In letting go of life
we discover new life

In accepting the inevitability of death,
we discover a new way of living

Reflecting on the brokenness and fragility of our day,
we go forward in a spirit of quiet attentiveness,
greeting the silence of descending dark

Trusting ourselves to the universe,
things go well

Not trusting,
we make ourselves orphans in an alien world

Ours is the choice:
to live in trust
or to live in fear

Each day, each moment,
I am one with the force of life
and I am passing away

We can overcome our fear
only by letting go of it

Attachment throws us off balance,
takes over our minds and hearts

Absorbed in ourselves,
we are unaware of what life is offering,
we are unable to receive
the joys of the moment,
the gifts of the day

Letting go,
we open ourselves
to receive what is given

Detachment:
accepting life,
accepting ourselves as we are,
accepting our giftedness
as well as our limitations

As we move towards death,
we grow into it,
day by day

Entering into the night
we return into the silence
that is the dark soil
in which we are rooted

The less we have,
the easier it is to appreciate what we have

Receptivity is a condition of the night

If we learn to die during life,
then, when our last hour comes,
we will be able to die easily

Detachment leads us out, beyond ourselves,
and connects us into the universe

The moment when we die to ourselves
is the moment we become fully alive

Indecision,
holding back,
standing on the edge of fear
brings no security

We die while we are alive

Bonded to the earth,
we watch how the dead, dark soil,
cold and silent,
waits
for the opening
out of which comes the new,
sprouting, budding,
blossoming and fruiting,
dying into seed
that goes once more into the cold and silent earth,
to sprout and bud
and blossom and fruit
and seed again

The word that we are
is always in the process of being spoken
It is completed only in death

When we live a detached life,
not pretending to be something we are not,
not seduced by things that protect us
from the truth about ourselves,
then we can live at ease with ourselves

Six inches apart
their eyes deliberately gazing into the heavens,
another sod is turned over them and the next
    ridge begins,
and ridge after ridge, row after row,
the potatoes are set

By nightfall, the brown field is turned over to God

When I accept my weakness
everything changes

The mirage of control disappears
and my weakness becomes my strength

Night completes the circle of the hours
as death completes the circle of life

To let go,
to be able to stand and leave everything behind
without looking back,
is to say yes:
inner freedom

Life is a river
If we learn to let go,
not clinging to the banks in fear,
we can go with the flow,
and life's river carries us,
bears us up in trust

Death is the way into the divine presence,
the resolution of a lifetime of wonder and waiting

Learning to be present to the present
in mindfulness and in recollection,
letting go of fear,
trusting the dark –
the beginning of serenity

When we rise wholeheartedly to the challenges
   of the day,
we will be able to let go
when it is time to leave it all behind,
as night falls

When we take water out of a river,
it's just a bucket full of water,
not the flowing river

By faith we die forward into fullness of life
and that is resurrection

Mothering is like dying:
the mother lets go of her child
so that the child can enter fully into life

In meditation we let go of everything –
the outer world of the senses,
the inner world of thought –
and listen to the still voice within

Darkness always finds us

Little deaths accepted
bring new life and inner peace

Knowing light shines in the dark,
we come to know darkness itself as light

In the midst of the ordinary,
joy is an experience of losing ourselves
of being emptied of self

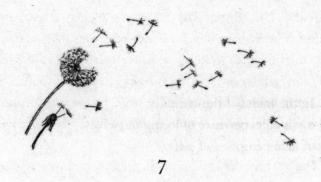

7

Speaking to the Creator

Prayer
Presence
Communion
Attuning us to the mystery of life

When anyone asks me how I pray, my simple answer is
that I rest in the presence of God. When I say God, I
mean a God who loves me, a God who is always there, a
God who knows me through and through. I expose to
God who I am and God gazes on me with the creative
and transforming eye of love. I believe God is the Eternal
Word who created and embraces heaven and earth and
reveals Him/Herself in different ways and under
different names and forms to all humanity.

Prayer is about presence, it is about being present in
the moment, in the now. In prayer there is no pretence,

no control, no glitter, no sham, just presence of heart and mind. The first steps in the dance of prayer involve finding the time and space to be present. It is not easy to be present in the now. We are usually ahead of ourselves or hanging behind. We are either stretching out to a future that is yet to come, or lost in the past that is no longer here.

Prayer is never private. Whatever is private excludes someone. Prayer is always an inclusive communion with God and with others. Everybody has different ways of making space for prayer in their lives. I find it helpful to allocate particular times for prayer. Times I set aside just to be alone with God. This requires discipline. It is an attitude that expresses my desire to pray.

I like to pray early in the morning and I like to start with a preparatory ritual. Usually I take off my shoes, pull back my curtains, even if it is still dark, and lay down a mat. I light a candle and remind myself that I am entering a place and space where I am alone with myself and my God. The very simple acts of pulling back the curtains and lighting the candle are part of my prayer ritual because they help me to recognize with my eyes, my mind and my heart that I am in the presence of greatness and goodness, in the presence of God, whatever way that goodness and greatness and presence speak to me.

When I find it difficult to quieten down and be present to God I use my breath to slow down my mind and body, to help me move into that quiet space within me where God dwells.

Prayer is the divine taking possession of us. We never achieve prayer; it is always received as a gift. And if we are prepared to pray, to lift our hearts and souls and minds to God, we develop an attitude of heart that can transform every aspect of our lives.

Time in prayer and meditation is very important to me. It helps me to refocus on the truly significant things of life. It helps me to find God in day-to-day life, in the midst of noise and distractions of all sorts, of pain and suffering and death, as in times of peace and quiet and of joy, happiness and friendship.

Prayer opens the heart and mind to God; that is, it goes beyond all the limited processes of the rational mind. Prayer opens the mind to the transcendent. Prayer is self-surrender. As long as we remain on the level of the rational mind, we are governed by our ego, our independent, rational self. In surrendering the ego, the separate self, and in turning to God, the supreme Spirit, we receive the light which we need to understand the deeper meaning of the mystery of life.

Prayer is a way of attuning ourselves to the flow
  of life

Sitting still,
trying not to try,
wanting not to want,
not setting my heart on anything,
I may accidentally discover that I am changed

Angelus bells –
mindfulness time,
sanctified by generations of people
lifting up their hearts to mystery

Prayer changes us
and in changing us
it changes the world

When I stop I find you
When I look I see you
When I listen I hear you

Prayer is not a question of straining the mind:
it is a simple matter of opening the heart

This is how we learn to be still:
by sitting quietly,
facing fear with trust,
listening to our own depth,
waiting for growth to happen,
allowing the dawn to rise out of the night

Peace is found not only in the desert
or in remote and silent monasteries
but in the tumult of the market place
and the pulse of the human heart

Creator of this ever-evolving cosmos,
where nothing is static,
you are the eternal energy of change

In you all things are made new

In you all things pass away

In you all things are brought to completion

Prayer is never a private matter
It is always inclusive,
as we open our hearts to the universe

You are the source of my being,
the spring feeding the river of my life
I am seeking you without knowing it,
encountering you without recognizing you,
stumbling upon you without seeing you,
held by you without fully trusting you

In God is my beginning and my end

Stillness accepts noise,
moves beneath it,
to an inner silence

You are always around me,
always sheltering me,
but it is only in awareness that I experience you

We are one, you and I,
bound together in a covenant of peace,
ringed around in a circle of love

You are always shaping us,
creating us in your likeness

Silently listening to our breathing,
we are intimately at one with the life breath of the
   universe

Deep in our heart we are alone

Teach me your ways,
so that I may hear you in silence,
see you in emptiness,
taste you in the fruits of the earth,
touch you in the gifts of creation

When we are too busy to be still,
our ears and eyes are open
only to our projects and plans,
and so we miss the wonder of the moment
that leads to truth

Forgiveness is a taste of divine grace – pure gift

You call out to me in the depth of my soul
You transform me into yourself
I live in you, with you, through you and by you

The vulnerable power of weakness
is a gift of the universe

Preserving the silence within
amid all the noise and clatter of life,
we grow into our true selves

Prayer is an opening of the heart
that takes us beyond
our limited rational mind,
beyond the ego and the separate self,
into the transcendent mystery

We are dust and earth and the breath of God

Within,
at the centre of my being,
in the recess of my soul,
in the deep marrow of my bone,
there is an unquenchable fire,
a gnawing desire,
a restlessness,
an aching longing,
a deep hunger,
which cannot rest or be satisfied
except in God –
and She is within

Faith is the eternal yes to the universe

O Holy One,
keep me in your sight,
let me not flee from your gaze

God is in the mountain
The mountain is in God

I am in the mountain
and the mountain is in me

Standing at the kitchen table,
she is totally absorbed in the mixing and kneading,
in the turning and folding,
as if this was the first bread ever made

Rounding and flattening it,
she makes the sign of the cross with the bread knife:
Father, Son and Holy Spirit

Then, taking it in her hands,
she raises it up and places it in the waiting pan

This is my body
Yes
I am

The soul of the world
is the pulse of the unfathomable,
the heartbeat of all creation,
mysterious,
sacred beyond words

Morning prayer
I have been spared another night
to come to this new dawn

Through you I rise
and you through me
into this new day
we are making together

Morning blesses us with time and space to be attentive
to all that is new this day

Morning prayer says very simply
and with deep faith, hope and love
good morning,
good morning,
good morning

Midday,
God's forgiveness flows through us,
bringing peace

Afternoon,
enthusiasm flagging,
crises looming –

The challenges of the day overwhelm us,
remind us to stop,
call us to reflect,
to catch our breath,
make peace,
find joy,
take rest,
find strength in the moment

Evening,
When we have forgotten how to pray
and prayer seems empty of meaning,
it is enough simply to surrender
and give ourselves over, in trust,
to the night

In night prayer
we connect the end of the day
with the end of life

Before we sleep,
gathering up all the day's contradictions,
knitting together what is broken –
a healing experience

Night,
a time to pray for peace
a time to trust the dark
a time to merge with the divine mystery

About the author

SISTER STANISLAUS KENNEDY is an Irish Sister of Charity and the founder and life-president of Focus Ireland. She is also founder and director of the Immigrant Council of Ireland, Young Social Innovators and the Sanctuary, a place of peace and stillness in the heart of Dublin.

She has been instrumental in developing and implementing social-service programmes that have benefited thousands of people in need throughout Ireland and Europe. For this work, she has received many awards, including Honorary Degrees of Law from Trinity College Dublin, the National University of Ireland and the Open University. She has also received a presidential medal from New York University and a prestigious Meteor Humanitarian Award.

She has written four bestselling books, *Now Is the Time*, *Gardening the Soul*, *Seasons of the Day* and *Stillness through My Prayers*.

Gardening the Soul
Soothing Seasonal Thoughts for Jaded Modern Souls
by Sister Stan

The *Irish Times* Spiritual Book of the Year, 2002

Sister Stan, as she is affectionately known, was brought up on a farm in Lispole in the Dingle Peninsula, County Kerry, one of the most beautiful parts of Ireland. It was there that she learnt to appreciate the earth, its stillness and its energy, its beauty and its bounty.

In this hugely powerful and evocative book, Sister Stan looks to the earth that is so precious to our existence for inspiration throughout the year. Reflecting the garden's changing rhythms through the seasons, *Gardening the Soul* offers us a daily thought to keep us going as we face the challenges of modern life.

All our moods are covered here . . .

* in January, when there is silence in the garden, she looks at Solitude in our soul . . .
* in March, with emergence in the garden, she offers Hope . . .
* in August, when there is fullness and abundance everywhere, there is Blessing, and
* in October, the time of harvest, there is Harmony

Comforting and insightful, *Gardening the Soul* is an inspirational daybook of lessons gleaned from the wisdom of nature.

Published by Transworld Ireland
9781848270640

Seasons of the Day
A Book of Hours
by Sister Stan

Based on the traditional *Book of Hours* – psalms said daily, at set times, by religious communities throughout the world – *Seasons of the Day* reveals the enduring relevance of this ancient practice to contemporary living.

In *Seasons of the Day*, Sister Stan, knowing that our modern-day understanding of time pushes us to our stressed-out limits, passes on the monastic ritual to the layperson.

Here, as she slows us down, she reveals the psalms through her own words, her own prayers. Using them, she also guides us tenderly through a four-week period, from the silence and mystery of pre-dawn (matins) through to the reflective conclusion of the day (compline).

In a world that can often seem hostile and unfriendly, her gentle reflections help the reader find inner peace and confidence.

A prayer book for today.

Published by Transworld Ireland
9781848270626

Now Is the Time
Spiritual Reflections
by Sister Stan

Now Is the Time became an instant bestseller when it was first published, and it has continued to sell to an increasing and eager audience who admire and understand Stan's way. In this expanded edition, which includes five new entries, Stan's message remains the same: we have the time, if we make the choice to take time . . .

Now Is the Time is a book for everyone; young or old, male or female, for the converted or those who are irreligious or plain disaffected. Even people for whom a spiritual view of the world is a closed book should try opening this one.

Now Is the Time looks beyond the boundaries of any one faith or church and draws on the great spiritual and philosophical traditions of East and West. As Sister Stan focuses on a line of poetry from one of the world's great authors, an idea from a psychotherapist or philosopher, or a proverb from oriental wisdom, she weaves her own thoughts around them in a way that presents them afresh, and allows us to see them from a new perspective.

Published by Transworld Ireland
9781848270633

Stillness through My Prayers
by Sister Stan

Stillness: A deep silence and quiet calm, bringing feelings of peace, solace, contentment and serenity.

You may need this book
if you have ever felt afraid, unsure, anxious or uncertain . . .

You may need this book
if you have ever had sleepless nights, feared the morning, faced difficult decisions, felt worried about the future or craved an answer to life's many mysteries . . .

You may need this book
if you are on a journey of self-discovery . . .

You may need this book
to start to trust and accept, to forgive and let go, with love and peace.

You may need to rest, to pause or stop

You may need this book
if you want stillness

In *Stillness through My Prayers*, Sister Stan shares simple, profound and calming prayers that she herself uses to help her achieve *Stillness* – that most elusive and treasured state of mind.

Published by Transworld Ireland
9781848270619